WRITINGS ON THE WALL

Reflections on the Vietnam Veterans Memorial

Compiled by Jan Scruggs, Esq.

Cover photo by Larry Powell

THIS BOOK IS DEDICATED TO
LEWIS BURWELL PULLER
1945–1994

Lewis Puller served his country bravely in the Vietnam War and was severely wounded. He was a great Marine, a Pulitzer Prize winning author, a talented attorney and a loving husband and father. He died in 1994 and will be missed by all.

FOREWORD

The Vietnam Veterans Memorial, The Wall, has become the most visited memorial in Washington, DC. Dedicated in 1982, this impressive tribute has done much to heal the wounds of our nation's Vietnam veterans.

Additions to the Memorial have taken place since 1982. In 1984 a statue of the Three Servicemen was placed near the West Wall and a flag added to the entry walkway. In November 1993, a statue was placed on the Memorial grounds honoring the women who served in Vietnam.

Much has happened since 1982. Indeed a new generation of Americans is now visiting and discovering this magnificent piece of architecture.

Some now visiting the Memorial were not born when construction was ongoing. They touch it. They walk its length. They think. They wonder . . . about the sadness they see there . . . the respect they see there . . . about the pride they see. Young people who visit wonder about history and how they were affected by events and times so distant.

Young Americans who now visit and future generations who will visit this Wall know this Memorial makes real that which may have been forgotten by history. They know this because the names of over 58,000 great American patriots are displayed. Americans who were once young. Who once wondered.

A nation comes to the Memorial to help heal its wounds. These two walls serve as the physical embodiment of a healing process which takes time, effort and understanding.

For many veterans, the cathartic effects of this Memorial have helped. Through this Memorial many veterans have met with their friends from the war. Part of the healing that the Memorial embodies is the knowledge among Vietnam veterans that their service has been recognized. For the Vietnam Veterans Memorial was built through private contributions from the American people.

Many hundreds of thousands of Americans donated the funds needed in order to get the Memorial built. Since 1982, many more have continued to donate to help maintain the Memorial and support the important educational activities carried out by the Vietnam Veterans Memorial Fund.

Just as the Memorial has helped to heal in the past, so must it help us to heal in the future. By standing as a symbol to communicate the lessons of history, future generations will be well served by "The Wall."

Timeline

1979 - Vietnam Veterans Memorial Fund (VVMF) formed.

1982 - VVMF builds and dedicates Vietnam Veterans Memorial.

VVMF holds first Veterans Day ceremony at the Wall, to be followed annually by Memorial and Veterans Day ceremonies in honor and memory of those who served.

1983 - VVMF adds 68 names to the Wall.

VVMF contracts extensive landscaping job at Memorial and installs walkway.

1984 - VVMF adds 15 names to the Wall.

VVMF installs lighting system.

Three Servicemen Statue and flag pole dedicated.

U.S. Postal Service issues stamp commemorating the Memorial.

1985 - VVMF forms Structural Advisory Committee to study cracks and structural integrity of the Memorial.

1986 - VVMF adds 110 names to the Wall.

1987 - VVMF adds 24 names to the Wall.

1989 - VVMF imports extra granite panels to be stored at Quantico Marine Base.

VVMF adds 19 names to the Wall.

1991 - VVMF begins plans for 10th Anniversary Commemoration.

VVMF adds 8 names to the Wall.

1992 - VVMF constructs new granite walkway.

10th Anniversary of Memorial is commemorated with year-long observance including educational seminars, VVMF concert, meal for Homeless Veterans, Vietnam War art exhibit, Reunion '92, etc. commencing with 60-hour Reading of the Names leading up to Veterans Day ceremony.

1993 - VVMF adds 8 names to the Wall.

Vietnam Women's Memorial Project dedicates Vietnam Women's Memorial on Veterans Day.

1994 - VVMF hires engineering firm to begin first phase of three-part study to determine the Memorial's future and long-term maintenance needs.

U.S. Mint issues silver dollar commemorating the Memorial.

Table of Contents

BOOKMARKS AND BEST FRIENDS

Phil Straw, Vietnam Veteran
University Honors Program
University of Maryland

Within the first hour of the initial session of Honors 318 (America in Vietnam) at the University of Maryland each year, a handmade manila bookmark—with a ribbon attached and an individual's name neatly inscribed upon it—is distributed to every student enrolled in the course.

The names are diverse, all printed by hand in ink. They've been selected with care and reason from the polished granite walls of the Vietnam Veterans Memorial.

They are the names—Mullen, Graham, Capodanno, Buis, Lane, Cushman, Atterberry, Sijan, Dodge and Duffey, and many others—of the best and brightest of a generation of can-do idealists who became in the moving, powerful words of author Joe Galloway, the down payment on JFK's promise to ". . . pay any price, bear any burden . . . ."

Each student is simply informed at the outset of the semester: this bookmark includes the name of your "best friend." They have to assume. Keep it, they are told. Use it, remember them as you attempt to understand this bitter and bloody war.

As the course unfolds, the students learn from stories I relate about our best friends — all killed in Vietnam, all hopeful once, not asking what their country could do for them.

They discover that Cushman was an Olympic medalist and a pilot lost over the North; that Lane was a devoted nurse committed to healing and helping, one of eight women listed on the Memorial; that Dodge was an outstanding first baseman, then a prisoner pictured on the cover of LIFE.

They learn that Sijan and Atterberry had been captives who tried to escape; that engaging Jerry Duffey from Michigan was the only American killed during one week of the war in 1972 and that Buis was among the first to die in an undeclared, agonizing Asian war which would eventually claim more than 58,000 American lives. His name is easy to find: it's at the apex of the Memorial.

Father Capodanno was a priest, a non-combatant and Graham was a Marine from Maryland awarded the Medal of Honor posthumously. His widow joins us in class on the evening we talk about his gallant efforts to save another Marine.

Michael Mullen was an Iowa farmer's son, killed by friendly fire. His mother, Peg, has never fully recovered and my students will never forget the war which took her son and changed her life.

Each name, you see, has dimension and worth, the students are told as the bookmarks are handed out on the first night of class. Except for another time and place, the person on the bookmark was just like you are now: bright, focused, a missionary in their own way.

If you were to meet them all individually—all of those killed in the war and remembered on the Memorial—at the rate of 10 a day, it would take 15 years.

We have an obligation to remember those who died in Vietnam, and to do so fittingly, with permanence. The Memorial allows us to do that.

It is a beginning and an end, a place from which to start writing names on bookmarks to be given to college students and a treasured place to end the journey for those who find comfort, peace and honor in the names of friends etched forever on a Memorial they deserve and we, the living, need.

(Ed. Note: Phil Straw, a Marine Corps infantry officer who was awarded a Purple Heart and Bronze Star with "V" while serving in the 3rd Marine Division in Vietnam in 1968-69, originated an honors course in 1985 at the University of Maryland to provide students a comprehensive examination of the causes and consequences of American involvement in Southeast Asia. An address delivered by a student in that honors program is included elsewhere in this book.)

Random Observations and Comments I

David E. Bonior, U.S. Representative (D-MI)

On a rainy day last March, I spoke at the ceremony commemorating the 10th Anniversary of the groundbreaking for the Vietnam Veterans Memorial.

Honored as I was, the greatest honor came afterward: tracing the names of two outstanding Americans from my home area—Daniel Cahill and Gerald Mullin—killed in Vietnam, their lives ended almost before they began.

How could this memorial have once been the focal point of such controversy? It is now the most revered monument in Washington.

Americans like Daniel Cahill and Gerald Mullin now live on not only in the memories of their families and friends—but in the granite walls of this memorial, which simply by listing their names has helped heal wounds that divided a generation.

The job is not complete. My hope is that as the years move along, this monument will continue to play its healing role and will continue to be the place above all others, where America remembers the sacrifice of those who served their country with such courage.

Hugh Sidey, Journalist

How splendid it has been in its humility and earthly dignity. A marble [granite] incision in the sacred soil of the Washington Mall. Beneath the gaze of Abraham Lincoln and Thomas Jefferson, in the shadow of the monument to George Washington and only a bugle call from Ulysses Grant, the warrior. Hate was buried in this tender furrow. Honor was reclaimed. Those named on that Wall who died in the Vietnam War now march in this country's caravan of the great.

Rose Lee, National President of Gold Star Wives of America

The Vietnam Veterans Memorial is especially meaningful to Gold Star Wives of America, Inc. This powerful memorial has the names of the husbands of many of our members.

One member's daughter named Amantha wrote a poem, ''The Big Black Wall.'' Her poem was dedicated to her father, John R. Hagood, a name on the big black wall. Amantha never knew her father—he died the same year she was born—1969.

The Wall has become a symbol, not only for the Vietnam War, but for other wars as well. Melinda Pesce of Everett, Massachusetts, sent me a letter with a poem.

Melinda's husband was killed in action during World War II, in 1944, the year their daughter Maria was born. Like Amantha, Maria wrote a poem about the father she never met. Maria's brother visited the Wall last Veterans' Day and left Maria's poem at the Wall.

At the end of the poem, she wrote, "For all children, who have lost parents serving their country in all wars and conflicts."

So you see why I think this Wall has taken on a meaning beyond a memorial for Vietnam veterans. This memorial has become a unifying symbol for all who have died in war. Maria has demonstrated that this Wall has meaning to survivors from other wars, too.

The meaning of the Wall has become enlarged. It is a real coming together. People are proud to be associated with this memorial.

It's okay to be a Vietnam Veteran, and we thank you.

Sarah McClendon, Journalist

Americans may never find out exactly why they were called to fight the Vietnam War. However, the uncovering of the various maneuvers that led to it in diplomatic and political and power-hungry circles are beginning to be unveiled.

As the people learn more about how they were manipulated, both the opponents and the supporters, it is hoped that they will ask questions before they submit to the slaughter of war.

Americans are ready at all times to defend their country. However, they are learning more and more about how secret diplomacy can involve them in needless wars as in the past.

In this war, many civilian employees of the government, especially the Central Intelligence Agency, were operating in positions of authority in Vietnam, often interfering with the plans and purposes of the experienced military. Why?

The unfairness of the selective service in excusing many from combat services while requiring that many poor and blacks who could not go to college and get deferments be enrolled to fight was a rank injustice.

Let us hope that Americans do not ever face such manipulations behind the scenes of powerful persons who glorify their misguided purposes as a holy war.

Elliott Richardson, former U.S. Attorney General

For me, the Vietnam Veterans Memorial carried a message at three levels.

On one level it signifies this nation's readiness to sacrifice in the cause of freedom. Although the Wall's dark marble [granite] may reflect doubts as to the wisdom of the sacrifices it records, it proudly affirms their nobility.

On a second level, the Wall perpetuates the memory of those who gave their lives in Vietnam. That is its role as a Memorial. It thus renews for succeeding generations both awareness of these sacrifices and gratitude for them.

The third level drives home the realization that those were <u>individuals</u> who died on the other side of the world: one by one, name by name—fathers, sons, brothers, uncles, cousins, neighbors, friends—all loved and valued no less than we ourselves.

James A. Baker, III, former U.S. Secretary of State

Ten years ago, the Vietnam Veterans Memorial was constructed amidst controversy and anguish. But in the course of that decade, it became a symbol of reconciliation, not division, of a reborn national will, not to forget, but to forgive and remember.

The austere simplicity of the roll call on that wall tells the story of individual American sacrifice—an indisputable sacred memory of those who paid the highest price for freedom.

The Wall is barely visible from the upper floors of the State Department, yet it can never be far from the gaze of our diplomats. As Secretary of State, it reminded me that the American people are willing to sacrifice, but their government has the duty to weigh its choices carefully and consider the consequences before risking American lives. This is, and must be, the firm conviction of every post Vietnam War generation.

While the Vietnam Wall still stands, another wall, the Berlin Wall, has fallen. There is new hope for a better world. And the Vietnam Wall should symbolize not the division among us, but the strength of our reconciliation and unity.

Those on the Wall, those heroes cast in bronze, would accept no less.

J. Carter Brown, Chairman of the Commission on Fine Arts

The Commission on Fine Arts is proud to have been involved in the Vietnam Veterans Memorial. Maya Lin's design is one of the most poetic and moving to have been created by an American in this century. The artistic quality of Frederick Hart's sculpture is also extremely high. No one can visit this great memorial without being enlightened, moved and proud.

Speech by Sarah Dwyer at the Vietnam Veterans Memorial, Veterans Day 1991

Please listen carefully to these words:

There is a destiny which makes us sisters and
   brothers,
None of us goes our way alone
For what you put into the lives of others,
Will—someday—come back into your own.

I am nineteen years old, the average age of a combat soldier in Vietnam. As my family would say, I wasn't even thought of during the Tet offensive and the siege of Khe Sanh. I was only a year old when the POWs came home and I was three when Saigon fell.

My name is Sarah Dwyer and I feel privileged to be here on Veterans Day, a special day of remembrance. I am a University of Maryland sophomore in a comprehensive Honors course to understand the causes and consequences of America's longest, costliest, most complex and mysterious war: Vietnam.

I speak today not with one voice but in harmony with the voices of my classmates and our generation. This message is from us, to you: to those who created the history we study in Honors 318:

WELCOME HOME
WELCOME HOME . . . AND WELL DONE

Thank you for this unique opportunity. The word veteran comes from the Latin word for "experience." And although our experiences differ greatly, we are honored to honor you . . . to join, if you will, even momentarily, the family of those who call themselves "veterans."

The generation before you passed on a promise: to defend this country. And although that promise was hard to keep, you did. And we, the generation that follows you, love you for it. You didn't ask in 1966 or '68 or '70 what your country could do for you.

Instead, you risked your young lives to make certain that people like me and a generation like mine can live freely in a country like this.

We—my fellow students and I—want you to understand that we "know" you and we value your service, sacrifice and sincerity.

We know WHO you are: the best and the brightest, doers and dreamers; you are soldiers, sailors, Marines, pilots, engineers, nurses, corpsmen, FO's and advisors, grunts and chaplains.

We know WHERE you served: An Hoa, Danang, Con Thien, Cam Ranh Bay, the Ashau Valley, Dong Ha, Quang Tri, Pleiku, from the Delta to the DMZ.

We know WHEN you served and most important of all, we know that you were asked to "pay any price . . . bear any burden."

Those in Honors 318 will never forget. Never. My generation is just one click—an academic firebase—behind you and we are eager to have you tell us more.

As our teacher, who is a Marine Corps veteran of Vietnam, has often said: all of you are teachers. For you have an obligation to teach just as much as we have an obligation to learn.

Our teacher has also said that you must touch the heart before you can teach the mind. You have touched our hearts, so please teach our minds. You have so much to give, so much to say, so much to invest in the goodness of a great nation.

The names listed on the long walls behind me were your best friends. They are ours as well. Every student who has taken 318 - every one— knows one name on this Wall.

We have not met them, but we know them because we learn about each one and their courage individually. We know who they were—good Americans like Capodanno, Cushman, Dugan, Atterberry, Sijan, Graham and Lane.

Once upon a time, they were young, too. Today,

we assemble here, and touch the names of our best friends on this angle of polished reflective stone, the Vietnam Veterans Memorial. We remember them.

There are actually two Memorials to Vietnam and to you at Maryland. Previous Honors 318 students dedicated an oak tree and a stone marker near the Chapel. The other memorial to understanding Vietnam meets each Tuesday and is given its life by young people like me — math and journalism majors, pre-med, engineers, and future attorneys, educators, architects and accountants. All builders.

In 1961, John Kennedy said that "the torch has been passed to a new generation of Americans — unwilling to witness or permit the slow undoing of those human rights to which this nation has always been devoted . . . "

You have served this nation and the legacy of that challenge well. Today, we willingly grasp that torch with you, and we thank you for keeping it aloft and lit for all to see.

We remember.

Speech by Jack Smith at the Vietnam Veterans Memorial, Memorial Day 1994

I want to talk about healing. Not only is it what this place is all about, but this ceremony, as you heard from Jan, is dedicated to Lew Puller and healing is apparently what Lew found too little of.

As Joe Galloway told you, I served in one of the most vicious fights of the Vietnam War in the Ia Drang Valley. My battalion was overrun. My company was cut to pieces. We sustained, I think I calculated, 90, 93 percent casualties in a day and a night of hand-to-hand combat. All my buddies, all the buddies I had in the world, I watched them die horribly, and that sort of thing, you can imagine, leaves scars behind.

For years afterwards, I was sour on life as a result. Bitter, cynical, alienated. But time heals and one day I woke up and I saw the world as I believe it really is, a bright and warm place. I looked at my scars and I marveled—I marveled not at the weakness of human flesh, my flesh, but at the indomitable strength of the human spirit. In spite of bullets, in spite of hot metal fragments, the spirit lives on. This is the miracle of life.

I don't know how much Lew's death had to do with Vietnam. I don't know how much of it had to do with Lew himself. But his death quickly came to symbolize all the loose ends of the war. I was haunted by another ghost, another loose end, one that haunts us all, all Vietnam veterans.

We won every battle, but the North Vietnamese, in the end, took Saigon. What on earth had we been doing there? Was all that pain and suffering worth it or was it just a terrible waste of time? This, I think, is why Vietnam veterans don't really let go, why many can't get on with their lives, what sets them apart from other veterans of other wars.

We got our parades and we finally built this Wall, this magnificent monument. That helped. But I know a number of my friends were still haunted by the futility of the war.

Then five years ago, I watched the Berlin Wall come down and, as an ABC News correspondent, I witnessed firsthand on a number of trips the collapse of communism. Containment, my friends, worked. We won the cold war. And however meaningless Vietnam seemed at the time, it contributed to the fall of communism. That was something to hold on to. Pretty thin, not very satisfying as a justification for what I and some of my friends went through in Vietnam, but it was something.

As you heard Joe tell, last year I returned to
Vietnam and it was there that I finally came to a
better understanding of the war that I fought in.
With my old commanding officer—Joe was there,
too, a group of other Ia Drang veterans—I traveled
to the jungle in the Central Highlands and I walked
the battlefield for two days in the company of some
of the North Vietnamese that we fought against
nearly 30 years ago. And it was an expérience I
shall never forget.

Did I find the answer to my question about the
futility of war? No. I don't know if what I did in
the war was worth it. But what I did find surprised
me.

The Vietnamese government, my friends, may
have conquered the South, but I can report to you
that it is losing the peace. The country is going
capitalist as fast as it can. What is General Giap
going to say to his grandson one day when he
comes home and says, "Grandpa, I just got named
country representative for IBM?" It's going to
happen. Communism is dying over there.

More important, much more important, Vietnam is a country at peace. Because the North Vietnamese feel they won, they are not haunted by the
same ghosts as we. And most of the people in the
South were born after the war, and so they don't
care. English over there is becoming the second
language. People wave and smile at you. They
liked us. And they could not understand what we

were doing over there, what ghosts we were trying to exorcise because they don't have those ghosts.

What struck me was the overwhelming peacefulness of the place, even the landing zone where I fought. I wanted to bring back some shrapnel or shell casings to lay here at the Wall under Panel No. 3, where all my buddies' names are, the total of more than 200. But, you know, I could not find any battle debris. Nature had simply erased it. And where once the ground, the elephant grass had been running with blood, there were flowers blooming in that place. It was—it was beautiful and still, and so I had to press some flowers and I brought those back. That's all I could find.

To come to terms with Vietnam means ultimately letting go. To make, as my friend Joe Galloway put it so well, Vietnam become a place again and not a war, as it still is for so many veterans, and I guess as it still was for Lew. What I discovered in Vietnam is that the war is over; it certainly is for Vietnam and the Vietnamese. As I said on "Nightline" in January about Vietnam: "This land is at peace, and so should we be." And so should we be, my friends. Vietnam is a place, not a war, and I began letting go.

That is the realization I brought back from Vietnam last year and the one that I'm sharing with you today on this Memorial Day. Thank you and God bless you all.

Fifty Yards from the Wall . . .

John F. Sommer, Jr.
American Legion

A great deal has been written and stated about the Vietnam Veterans Memorial over the past 10 years. The Wall has been described in such varying terms as controversial, provocative, most visited, healing, reconciling, talismanic, to name a few.

My personal experience with feelings about the Wall have been similarly paradoxical. The week of the dedication involved a series of emotional events which shall not soon be forgotten.

During the ceremony itself, I watched from the southeast knoll about fifty yards from the Wall, which was as close as I got to it for a period of a year. My excitement at its existence was tempered by memories dredged up from 1968.

My first actual visit to the Wall was at daybreak, and the reverence felt at that moment was almost mystical. As I found, one by one, the names of my fallen comrades, it was if their presence was experienced. Hours passed before my retreat.

Then there were the occasions of bringing other combat vets to the Wall for the first time—the tears, the memories, and finally the serenity.

As time has passed, memories of friends like George who made it through Vietnam only to die of diseases like non-Hodgkins lymphoma are evoked when I visit, regardless of the fact that his/their names are not on the Wall.

Unfortunately, by the time that the long-term health effects of exposure to Agent Orange and other environmental factors are determined, there will be many more.

The one collective feature of the Wall which really raises my angst is the series of approximately 1,300 names denoted by a cross instead of a diamond—those who are listed as Prisoner of War/Missing in Action.

Too many years have passed and too little has been done. Our government and that of the Socialist Republic of Vietnam must reverse their past inaction and indiscretions, and immediately seek a full accounting of those who have yet to return.

In the meantime, much improvement must be effected in the way in which their families are being treated.

And speaking of families, that brings me full-circle—to end where this began. During this past Father's Day weekend, it was my honor to interact with some of the fine young people gathered in Washington for the first Sons and Daughters in Touch reunion.

The experience of facilitating a sharing group was moving to say the least. The emotion/pain/anger/love that had been bottled up in some for years was released and discussed by and with their peers.

The intensity of the feelings expressed was enormous. I was taken aback in hearing that a number of the Sons and Daughters were visiting the Memorial for the first time—and some were only able to get as close as the southeast knoll, probably about fifty yards from the Wall.

Random Observations and Comments II

G.V. (Sonny) Montgomery, Chairman of the U.S. House of Representatives Committee on Veterans' Affairs (D-MS)

As *Time* magazine put it, Vietnam was a war that "cost America its innocence and still haunts its conscience."

We owe an infinite debt of gratitude to those we asked to leave home, family, friends, and jobs to be thrust into the carnage, fear and uncertainty of a jungle on the other side of the world.

Their country asked and they went. It is with that same loyalty that we must embrace our Vietnam veterans and remember those who did not return.

America survived the divisive Vietnam era. We are still emerging from it in fact. Some events along the way salved the wounds it created and promoted healing, none more than the "thank you" expressed on the Washington Mall in November, 1982 . . . the Vietnam Veterans Memorial was dedicated.

Simple in design, yet complex in purpose, the Memorial has since become a symbol of America's increasing willingness to listen to those who survived the war and its desire to remember those who didn't.

The Vietnam Veterans Memorial gave the nation a way to offer its love and appreciation to some of our best and bravest.

More than just a structure to view or touch, it is an experience, a solemn and powerful place that you cannot walk away from; it and the warriors it honors remain in your heart, where they rightfully belong.

John Kerry, U.S. Senator (D-MA)

The Wall reminds us of the magnitude of suffering and sacrifice and of the bravery and commitment of those who served in America's most difficult and controversial war.

Behind each of almost 60,000 names, there is the story of a life cut short. Behind each, there is the face of a child growing up among us and being sent half way around the world to fight for us. Behind each, there are portraits of family, community and friends.

There is great depth to this smooth black Wall. You think you are touching it, but it is touching and teaching you.

I hope we will heed the lessons of this Wall by

honoring the dead, respecting the veteran and establishing the truth about those still missing.

I hope we will heed the lessons of this Wall by not avoiding future sacrifice, but by making ourselves worthy of <u>their</u> sacrifice; by confronting with honesty and boldness the social and economic problems we face; and by demanding from ourselves and from each other the fullest possible measure of service to community and country.

I hope we will heed the lessons of this Wall by remembering that although each of us may bring to it our own set of convictions, memories, prayers and personal pain; we must each strive to take from it a sense of larger purpose and perspective.

We must, in the name of those who paid the highest price for division, vow now to end division; and in the name of those who suffered most, work to complete the healing process and restore our nation and our people to their fullest strength.

Finally, I hope we will heed the lessons of this Wall by understanding when we visit this memorial that although there is no glory inherent in war, itself, there is dignity without measure in the memories we share, in the sacrifice we honor and in the prayers we offer.

So let those who have fallen rest. Let the drums of war cease. And let this sacred place inspire us and guide us for decades and decades to come.

Lionel Chetwynd, Writer and Producer

The names stand in mute sentinel, piling one upon the other in their tens of thousands, each representing a too-brief human passage.

Surely, even Death is embarrassed at the richness of the harvest; for these were, in so many ways, the best of us, the finest of who we are as a people. And certainly, none asked that this be their place in the history of the Nation.

Yet here they are, the names, etched in the perfect mirror of the black granite that reflects back the Mall and our great public shrines. They belong here. They bear terrible silent witness to the price of that now long-ago war.

It was not given to them to avoid battle or escape the demands their Country placed upon them. It was not given to them to remember those years as a political struggle fought on the streets of America's cities.

All that was allowed for them was to pay the price demanded.

And by doing so, they are our redemption. The Wall exists to immortalize those who fell, give succor and comfort to those who loved them, grant closure to those who served by their side, and no less importantly, say to those who chose to place themselves apart from the National Service, "Come closer, brother and sister.

We who fell can now sleep at peace for we shall

never be forgotten. Let us again be one people. Honor us by doing in our name what Death has prevented us from doing ourselves: be righteous stewards of our beloved country by bringing peace and justice to the land."

At the Wall we can all join hands, forgive one another, and know we are healed.

May God grant the fallen the perfect peace promised by his prophet Jeremiah, "I will give them an everlasting name that shall not be cut off." (Jer.56:5)

God Bless them and God Bless America.

Emogene Cupp, Gold Star Mother

The American Gold Star Mothers, Inc., founded in 1928, is an organization of women whose sons or daughters have given their lives in military service to our country.

My own son, Robert William Cupp, gave his life as an Army infantryman in Vietnam on June 6, 1968.

In 1979, I was National President of the American Gold Star Mothers when Jan Scruggs and Robert Doubek came to our National Headquarters in Washington, D.C., to explain Jan's idea of building a memorial to the Vietnam veterans.

I was so impressed with his idea that I volunteered to assist him in any way that I could. Later, I was privileged to unveil the first panel that was placed on the Wall.

All those whose names are inscribed on the Wall had a mother who bore them. You can see how many broken hearts have been honored by their son's or daughter's name being etched in the beautiful black marble [granite].

The Wall has been a source of healing for the mothers, as well as the veterans that served this country.

I wish every mother could come to see the Vietnam Veterans Memorial and experience the feeling that her son or daughter is remembered for their supreme sacrifice.

The Vietnam Veterans Memorial is now part of our national history and culture; thanks to Jan Scruggs, Robert Doubek, John Wheeler, many volunteers, and those who contributed the money.

It took teamwork to accomplish the task of building the most beautiful and visited monument in the city of Washington, D.C.

Bob Dole, U.S. Senator and Minority Leader (R-KS)

I am proud to salute our Vietnam veterans as we mark the 10th Anniversary of the Vietnam Veterans Memorial, the world famous Wall in Washington that has become such a poignant symbol of America's long and difficult conflict in Indochina.

Too often the valor of our fighting men and women in the jungles of Southeast Asia has been obscured by controversy and politics. The good news is, 1992 saw a long overdue recognition of our heroic Vietnam vets thanks to America's smashing victory in the Persian Gulf.

As our Desert Storm troops came home from the Middle East, America rejoiced at the sight of our Vietnam vets marching with them in the parades, taking their rightful place in the national spotlight for a job well done.

As millions of Americans come to Washington each year to tour the Nation's Capital, I am pleased that the Vietnam Veterans Memorial has become an essential stop for most visitors. It is a moving sight, a moving tribute and a moving force behind America's newfound respect and admiration for every single man and woman who served so honorably in Southeast Asia.

As a fellow veteran, I am proud to salute them all as we solemnly remember their sacrifice, especially those courageous Americans whose names we honor on the Wall.

John H. Chafee, U.S. Senator (R-RI)

The stillness of the Vietnam Veterans Memorial, and the clarity of the surface of the Wall, are as evocative to me of the faith that each of the 58,191 men and women who never returned from Vietnam had in their purpose.

As Secretary of the Navy during the final years of the Vietnam conflict, I know what courage it took for those fine young people not only to stare death in the face, but to do so knowing that a country they loved, for which they were prepared to die, did not uniformly support them.

It seemed when the Wall went up, that it set apart a time that the veterans of Vietnam felt abandoned by their country, from a time that they were embraced. This miraculous Wall has had the power to convince people who deeply opposed the war, that the war's soldiers were not indivisible from a policy they considered to be wrong, even immoral.

Instead, those whose names are etched in black granite are now known for who they were: individual Americans who loved their country so fervently that they answered the call.

No matter what historians decide about Vietnam, no one can deny that these individuals believed they were fighting to preserve the freedom that we enjoy today.

As I reflect upon the message of the Wall, I think how urgent it is that those of us who were lucky enough not to lose our lives in service to our country, or who have not been called upon to serve, honor the legacy of those who gave their lives in Vietnam.

In my view, the best way to repay the sacrifices

of our veterans is to vow never to take for granted
our responsibilities as citizens of the United States
of America.

We must fulfill our obligations as participants
in a democracy, and instill in our children the
values that make a democracy work.

That means we should vote on election day. We
should obey the law. We should speak up when
we notice the rights of our neighbors have been
infringed upon.

And, if we don't think the system is working,
if we don't like the way things are, then we should
roll up our sleeves and pitch in to change it for
the better.

Change is always possible. Look at how a simple Wall has transformed an entire nation.

Jim Bohannon, Mutual Radio
Talk Show Host

To me, the Wall has come to mean quiet, reflection and solitude. My working hours occasionally
put me there in the middle of the night.

I've walked that descending-ascending path on
more than a few early Sunday mornings, around
3 or 3:30. In between the Saturday night party-
crowd and the Sunday morning joggers,
Washington can be particularly moving. Nothing
is more moving than the Wall.

To be sure, there is great emotion to be felt in
broad daylight, as bearded, balding veterans place

medals and flags and letters there. But to me, that is spectacle.

The middle of the night . . . is healing. Even though I've never been there entirely alone, I've been alone enough: alone enough to pass by those names and note where mine might have gone, somewhere between April, 1967 and April 1968. Was there ever a bullet or a 122 millimeter rocket with my name on it, which wound up being marked, "Return to Sender, Address Unknown?" Was it misdelivered, to someone else . . . one of those names up there?

I've been alone enough to wonder about the luck of the draw. And then I leave, grateful to have been granted another dawn, just a few hours hence.

Richard Cheney, former Secretary of Defense

This memorial symbolizes America's appreciation for those who made the ultimate sacrifice on behalf of our nation in the Vietnam war, and for all who served.

Its granite panels record the dedication of Americans from every city and state—not only in the names that are inscribed, but also in the reflected faces of the friends and families who come to the Wall to remember and pay honor.

We are all indebted to the Vietnam Veterans and others whose efforts helped build and maintain the monument. The healing power of the memorial's quiet strength and beauty has made it a national treasure.

"We had no names. We had so many."

Lynda Van Devanter
Vietnam Veteran Nurse

We had no names. We had so many.

Most people who come to the Wall, come with a particular person in mind, a buddy, friend, or relative, someone who epitomizes the Vietnam war for that person.

For those of us who served in Vietnam caring for casualties of the war, our memories are of faces, stories, injuries — young kids those names became a blur of Billys, Gerrys, Smittys, Joses and Sammys.

In the years of healing from the war, there was frequently a sense of detachment, incompleteness. I recall thinking often during the time between the groundbreaking for the Wall, and the dedication, "But I haven't got any names."

I finally realized there were at least two names I could seek: a cousin who died while I was in Vietnam, and a nurse who was killed the day I arrived in Vietnam.

The day of the dedication I was prepared to look

for their names. What I was not prepared for was the powerful feelings the Wall would evoke in me. I did not make my search that day. I made many trips to the Wall before I gathered the courage to look up Steve and Sharon.

As I stood before their names, I became aware of the great distance between them. Nine panels filled with names separated them.

I found the panel containing the names from my last day in the war, and realized there were more than fourteen panels from my year in Vietnam. **Fourteen.** Thousands and thousands of names, many of which had been my patients over that long, tough year.

I could not remember any of their names, but they all looked familiar. In the hours, the weeks, the years I've spent by the panels, they've all become mine.

The memories, the lives, the kids—they all became mine. The war took them all away from me. The Wall gave them back.

I had no names. I have so many.

(Ed. note: This submission, originally solicited for inclusion in a 10th anniversary program was restricted to 250 words. Since space is not so limited now, it is thought that readers might find the cover letter that accompanied this piece interesting as well. It follows.)

You know, the Wall has such personal meaning

for me, that writing about its impact in only 250 words is darn hard.

I could have written about how the answers to my daughter's questions about, "what did you do in the war, Mommy," came more easily while sitting quietly with her at the Wall.

I could have written about the many friends who have come back together since the war, at the Wall.

I could have written about the last memories I have of my friend Jude who died last week of a brain tumor, and who was the subject of the poster we carried in 1984 while bringing our women Vietnam veterans wreath to lay at the Apex.

Jude was an ICU nurse at the 71st with us, and the sign read, "Women Vietnam veterans . . . . and Jude."

So I wrote what I wrote, and hope it's what you need. I wish you best, and if I can do anything more, just call.

Freedom, Healing, Challenge, Survival, Dreams

Brig. General George B. Price (Ret.)

When I think of the Vietnam Veterans Memorial, five words always come to mind: freedom, healing, challenge, survival and dreams.

First, freedom. The Vietnam Veterans Memorial freed many people of the repressed hostility they felt over the war and its result. It was and is a great catharsis for veterans and non-veterans alike. It also freed the country of the guilt over the way it pursued the war and made it better for those serving in Desert Storm. It also represents one of our most valuable freedoms, freedom of speech and the right to dissent. It gave America a salve for its conscience, a salve that would cure a serious wound.

Healing—The Vietnam Veterans Memorial fulfills this aspect of its role superbly at all levels—physical, emotional, mental and symbolical. It lets each visitor heal themselves while standing there making no statement at all. It satisfies the emotional needs of those who served, letting them know that their service was not in vain. It satisfies the mental along with the emotional by memorializing those whose sacrifice was the greatest.

It challenges those who served to work at forgiving those who did not so we can get on with what this great country is all about. It is a physical symbol to those who served that their comrades who died will never be forgotten.

Their names on the Wall are a tribute to us all. They remind us daily that we must learn from the lessons of this war. They are somebody and always will be.

It was best described by a friend of mine who said, "most walls are constructed to separate and divide people and nations. This is the only wall built to bring people together, to heal a nation."

Challenge—The Vietnam Veterans Memorial challenges us to make our country realize its full potential. If we are going to make the sacrifice of those who died worthwhile then we owe it to them to make our country move ahead and realize all that it can be in its new role as world leader.

Just as the construction of the Memorial was challenged on all sides, so is our country being challenged. We must continue to make a difference. The country withstood the third greatest challenge in its history, the first two being the Revolution and the Civil War. Now we must respond to the challenge presented by the new world order.

Survival—We have survived all of the challenges by those who wanted the Memorial to fail. This is in keeping with the rich tradition of our country. We have survived against overwhelming odds. We must continue to survive with the same innovative high energy effort that has brought us this far.

Dreams—The Memorial stands as visible evidence that dreams can come true. You can take great credit for this dream. It was yours and no praise is too high. Your contribution to our nation can only be measured in terms of the number of visitors to the Memorial. It says we thank you for letting us share your dream. It says thank you for feeling strongly enough about your dream to make it a reality.

If I added a sixth word, it would be fulfillment. Participation in the effort to get the memorial completed was the most fulfilling experience of my life. I feel fortunate for having had the experience.

In closing, I can still hear the words:

Stony the road we trod, bitter the chastening rod felt in the days when hope unborn had died.

Yet with a steady beat have not our weary feet strayed from the place for which our fathers died?

We have come over a way that with tears has been watered.

We have come treading a path through the blood of the slaughtered.

Out of the gloomy past till now we stand at last.

Where the bright gleam of our bright star is cast.

The Paradox of the Wall

Wanda Ruffin, Vietnam War Widow

When the Vietnam Veterans Memorial was dedicated in November 1982, I didn't want to attend the ceremonies. I had dealt with the loss of my husband who had been declared MIA in 1966 and KIA in 1974 (Body not Recovered), and my daughter and I were "going on with our lives."

But when I saw pictures of the Wall, I found myself searching the names, wondering if I would see that special name among the thousands. And I was moved by the emotional responses I observed in the eyes of those who were finding and touching their special name(s). But I didn't need to do that!

In 1983, when my husband's remains were finally returned to us, we selected Arlington National Cemetery as his burial site. While we were here, my daughter and I visited the Wall.

We were not prepared for the emotional impact, first of seeing all those names, and second, of finding and touching that name which held so much significance for us.

As we stood before Panel 5E and touched the name there on line 49, it was if my husband were standing there, and his name was engraved just above his head (he was 6'5'' tall.) We held each other and cried together as we were struck by the connection with his presence and the pain of his absence.

Thus began our paradox of the Wall and a healing journey which continues.

I moved to the DC area in 1985, but only visited the Wall upon requests from out-of-town visitors. It was always painful to touch the name, to read the letters, poems and pictures left there, and especially to see the tears on the faces of those who found names of loved ones and fallen comrades.

But my academic background in nursing and grief counseling provided the realization that not only were these letters, poems, and tears, tributes to those lost, they were also the symbols of catharsis and often, the beginning of healing.

Eventually, I came to see the Wall also as a point of connection as I directed the Vietnam Veterans Memorial's *In Touch* locator program which helps the friends, families and fellow veterans of those named on the Wall to find each other.

Sons and Daughters *In Touch*, our organization to connect those whose fathers were lost in Vietnam, has been especially significant in this concept.

On Father's Day, 1992, as over 300 Sons and Daughters *In Touch* gathered at the Wall to pay tribute to their fathers as well as to celebrate Father's Day with each other, I was again struck by the paradox.

As many of these young adults touched their father's name on the Wall for the first time, they shed tears of pain mixed with tears of joy. While their grief surfaced in the face of that black granite, so too were reflected the hugs of comfort for each other and the joy that they were not alone.

As I addressed this beautiful group of "living legacies of the Wall," I was also moved by the visual paradox: the Wall, the symbol of my life's greatest tragedy, yet because of the Wall, I was facing the symbol of our country's greatest hope for its future.

And these children, who had to experience the world's cruelty at such an early age, could now find their safe place of comfort and solace in the arms of the Wall.

Random Observations and Comments III

John Warner, U.S. Senator (R-VA)

For ten years, the souls of the thousands of men and women who gave their lives in this war have triumphed on this Wall. For ten years, this Wall has attested to the bravery and undying courage of these men and women.

This Wall has scorched into our collective consciousness the memory of these warriors, warning us of the agony which awaits if we should ever enter another such conflict. For ten years, it has introduced a new generation to the horrors of war.

It has soaked up the tears of a wounded nation as we grieve for those we have lost, and it has given those who survived a place to vanquish the terror in their past and heal their memories, if only for a moment.

During the past ten years, this Wall has helped a nation heal and for that we are grateful. No, we can never recover the laugh, the smile or the voice of those gentle warriors.

However, as each engraved name calls out to

its comrades and to all Americans, it proclaims the glory of an individual who selflessly loved his or her country.

It has often been said that something or someone cannot be all things to all people. Whoever uttered this now-famous line never experienced the Vietnam Veterans Memorial.

For ten years, this Wall has reflected and validated the entire spectrum of human emotion. Rage, desperation, pride, joy, comfort, understanding, hate, have all commingled among those who have approached this Wall.

I hope that all those who visit the Memorial will reach a peace with the past and secure a healing for the future, just as those immortalized on this Wall have found an everlasting peace.

Colonel Harry G. Summers, Jr., USA (Ret.), Editor, Vietnam Magazine

Ten years ago, they called it a "Black Gash of Shame," a "Hole in the Ground," a "Sarcophagus." The one thing that it was never called was a "Victory Monument." But as history continued to unfold, that's what it has turned out to be.

Victory in war is the attainment of the political objectives one sets out to achieve. While the military objectives were muddled and unclear, at the grand strategic level Vietnam was part of the larger struggle between communism and democracy. When Saigon fell, it was seen as a plus for communism and as a loss for democracy and the United States.

But Vietnam was just a battle in a much larger war, and the final victory of that war is now at hand. With the fall of the Berlin Wall and the breakup of the Soviet Union, it is Communism that finds itself on the ash heap of history. And it is democracy, and the United States, that has emerged as the ultimate victor in that epic struggle.

It is a world profoundly different from the one when the Vietnam Veterans Memorial was dedicated. And it is different in large measure because of the sacrifices made by those whose names are inscribed on the Wall. "Black Gash of Shame" indeed. How about "V" for Victory instead?

Chris Noel, Entertainer

Hi Luv, this is from Chris Noel.

When I first heard about our Vietnam Veterans Memorial, I could not get past the image of black walls sunk into the ground. Boy, was I wrong!

In 1966, I became the first woman to have my own radio show, "A DATE WITH CHRIS," on Armed Forces Radio Network. I read letters from Nam and music from the United States of America was played.

As a woman whose job was to raise morale by handshake tours and entertaining the troops in the field, firebases and hospitals of Vietnam, I wanted the Memorial to be white, tall and above ground. When I first saw the Memorial at the 1982 dedication, I was stunned by the impact of its power and beauty.

It has become the place for our Veteran families to meet when lonely and wanting to find peace in mind and soul. The Wall, a place for America to weep and to hug, kiss, smile and heal.

Our Wall is our place in America where we can finally all come together and love one another.

Let's finally feel that contentment in knowing we all did the best we could with our youth. Today let the Wall be the catalyst to let us dream—while we may!

Let's have one more day . . . to live . . . to give . . . to celebrate joy and know that we were SAVED TO SERVE!!

I love you—your Sister from Nam.

George J. Mitchell, U.S. Senator and Majority Leader (D-ME)

Ten years after the dedication of the Memorial is an appropriate time to reflect on the Wall, its message of reconciliation and its impact on our country.

It is especially timely now, as so many Americans are beginning to come to terms with the divisions that Vietnam created so many years ago, and to recognize that it is a shared national experience that reflects the idealism of all Americans—those who served, those who sought an earlier end to the conflict, and most important, those who led the way to national reconciliation by making the Memorial a reality.

Current hearings on the wrenching issue of prisoners and missing men are a reminder that the tragedy of this war was not only broad, but for all too many Americans, has lingered for many years since Americans left Southeast Asia.

There have been a number of important milestones in the history of the Vietnam Veterans Memorial: groundbreaking ceremonies in March 1982; the dedication of the Memorial on Veterans Day 1982; the transfer of the Memorial to the United States government two years later and the passage of legislation in 1990 to have a memorial honoring female Vietnam veterans located adjacent to the Wall.

At each and every step the Wall has served to heal the wounds of a nation and of those who fought the war and left friends there.

That experience takes place millions of times annually for Americans visiting the Memorial. For many of the 25 million Americans who come to the Wall each year, it is the most vivid, often the most powerful experience they have in the Nation's Capital.

This Memorial symbolizes the shared sorrow

of all those who served, those who returned and those who did not. It is no accident that the Wall is the most-visited site in the nation's capital: It is the most significant contemporary memorial to an American experience.

The Wall is also a belated gesture by a grateful nation to honor the service of the 58,191* men and women who gave their lives for freedom in Vietnam and the millions who served along side them and returned to take their rightful place in their communities.

It should cause all Americans to ponder the sacred obligation we have to those who wear this nation's uniform.

For if we are unable or unwilling to honor those who served in the past, we will be unable to summon those needed to serve in the future.

And so this memorial, which owes its existence almost exclusively to the veterans themselves, heals the wounds of the past, honors those who fell, and reconciles us to take up our nation's responsibilities in the future.

May God bless all those remembered here.

---

* as of Memorial Day 1993

"Silently We Commune"

Rick Miller, Vietnam Veteran

This is the final resting place for the spirits of my buddies, their names carved into rock. I'd like to say that I don't care where their bodies lie, but can't. This wall, this black granite, inscribed with endless names, is all that I have left of my Vietnam brothers—the ones who left their lives "over there."

I stare into the names through the blackness and see their faces—blank in death. Yet they are alive in spirit and as fresh in life as the day they left.

My buddies are right before me screaming the silent closed-mouth scream of death. I stand before them and they stand before me, this black sheet of granite the great dividing wall between the coming-home-me and the coming-home-them.

We touch hands through the Wall as touching through a glass window. I feel this tremendous energy pulling me into them and they to me. We silently remain buddies, respectful of the distance between us that can't be broken. They are prisoners within the earth, behind this Wall of black granite. Silently we commune.

I want to scream at everybody around me to get the hell out. "Leave, leave me alone in this graveyard—this is sacred ground." "Stop gawking, go away all you tourists."

I want to be alone with my buddies. I want to talk to them, in silence. I want to hear what they have to say. Tell me, buddies, tell me what you are thinking as you stare silently at me—into me.

"Go away tourists, this area is hallowed. I want to hear my buddies."

As I kneel before the Wall with tears slowly trickling down my cheeks, one woman wants to know if I had friends who served in Vietnam. I can't believe her rudeness. I wouldn't walk up to her as she knelt before a headstone in a cemetery and ask her if she knew the person.

Then another woman interrupts my world. There are too many tourists here. She asks if I was in Vietnam and tells me that her two brothers went "over there." I want to be nice to these people. I don't want to be rude. And this woman probably has understanding and real compassion. As I attempt to answer her my voice cracks and is lost. I return silently to my silent brothers behind the Wall.

This Wall, this memorial to those killed in Vietnam, is a graveyard and a tourist attraction. Go over to Arlington Cemetery and look at all the white tombstones. So, so many. By row and column, hill after hill. It has tremendous weight as you realize that all these men and women died in war for our country. All those bodies, once young and daring, obedient to the cause, lying in their boxes, decaying or decayed.

But in that cemetery, the tourists ignore all the common white markers and they visit the famous spots. Now, this black Wall is a condensed version of that cemetery and the tourists gawk here.

The black granite Wall is amass with names, endless. Three-dimensionally, the Wall rises from the ground and rears its mouth full of names. It is the giant earth monster that has gladly gobbled up soldiers.

And it smiles with all the names. Resting now, it records the lives lost in a conflict full of political conflict ten thousand miles away. The names, all those names, that is what this memorial is all about.

There is every kind of name imaginable—all nationalities of Americans. And behind every name is a face—a person and the spirit of that person.

The impact of this memorial is all those names, each with a face in the blackness of the stone. These names are real people, kids doing what they thought was right or what they had to do, mimicking their heroic forebears of Korea, the World Wars and the Civil War.

This Wall, standing sturdily, but shrouded in its blackness, is all that the lost have to show for their effort. Fifty-eight thousand one hundred ninety one faces. No victory, no defeated enemy, no conquered evil regimes. Only political hyperbole for and against. Vietnam, once a thousand miles long and nearby, is not one mile long and on the other side of the moon. 58,191 faces wanting to know if they accomplished something, if they did okay. 58,191 families and millions of friends wanting to know why. This Wall, this black granite, is the answer.

Go away tourists—let me release into the Wall and join my buddies.

As I stand before the Wall, I can feel the earth begin to tilt, slant downward to the Wall. I remain calm and motionless as my feet slowly begin to slide.

At last I am going—free. I can feel the wind in my face as my nose smells "over there." I am sliding faster, the wall flies to me and I fly through it. The sounds of Vietnam surround me and I can see them. Finally I am with them. My buddies, I am home at last.

Memorial Day 1994 Remarks on the Vietnam Women's Memorial

Dr. Elaine Niggemann, Vietnam Veteran
Army Nurse

Twenty five years ago in the midst of Vietnam, who among us would ever have dreamed that we would be here, at the Vietnam Veterans Memorial on Memorial Day, 1994?

When I went to Vietnam as an Army Nurse, less than a year out of college, the thought of a Vietnam Women's Memorial would have been beyond my wildest imagination.

Although I felt very wise and mature, in retrospect, I was really fairly young, very naive, and sometimes foolish. When I returned home, I was of course a year older, more mature and certainly wiser.

The wisdom I gained in Vietnam has continued to grow and mature with time, changing perspectives, and life's experiences, especially becoming a physician and a mother.

I was asked to comment on the meaning of the Vietnam Women's Memorial to myself, to the women who served during or in Vietnam, and to America. The easiest part of that assignment is to address what the Memorial means to myself.

First, it is a tribute and recognizes those women who served. We worked hard, we cared, and we sometimes cried. Much has been written about the emotional and physical trauma of Vietnam.

There were, however, positive aspects of the experience. My year in Vietnam was "growth-producing" to say the least. I acquired excellent nursing experience and assumed more responsibility than if I had remained in a stateside civilian nursing position.

More important than professional growth was personal growth. I discovered that despite our problems here in America we are very fortunate to live in a country with the freedom and opportunities we enjoy.

I discovered the excitement of travel to foreign countries and experiencing new cultures — just like my recruiter promised. As I met the daily challenges of my work in Vietnam, I discovered a sense of self-confidence and the value of perseverance.

Later, during some of the more demanding periods in medical school and residency, I found myself thinking, "if I can get through Vietnam, I can get through this."

It was in Vietnam that I discovered the frailty of human life — ours is a tenuous physical existence that continues to hold me in awe. Finally, I discovered the satisfaction of being able to make a difference by caring and doing the best I could.

It was a year filled with many discoveries and although I didn't appreciate it at the time, the experience has had a major impact on my life.

I am truly grateful for the opportunity to have served as an Army Nurse in Vietnam. I know the nurses, doctors, corpsmen, Medivac helicopter pilots, Red Cross, and all those involved in the medical care of the military made a difference.

I am proud of my contribution in Vietnam. When my three year old and five year old sons visit this Memorial someday, I want them to be proud of their Mom.

I think they will be, as this Memorial is a beautiful tribute to the women who served during Vietnam and recognition of hard work, devotion, and willingness to give of themselves.

I also believe that the Vietnam Women's Memorial, like this Wall, is a reminder to our country of the lessons we learned. We all know that peace and freedom have a high price.

In the Vietnam Women's Memorial, a wounded soldier is held in the arms of a nurse. I would go back again and be the nurse, but I don't ever want one of my sons to be that soldier.

We did learn lessons in Vietnam—let's remember them and let there be no more Walls.

This Memorial also says "women served."

Women have always served. There were women in World Wars I and II, Korea, Vietnam and Desert Storm. Wherever and whenever there were wounded soldiers, there were nurses.

The physical care, the concern, and the compassion of a nurse are irreplaceable. Many women fulfilled many roles in Vietnam. The strong yet tender and caring qualities of women are portrayed on the faces of the women in the Vietnam Women's Memorial.

This Memorial reminds our country that women did indeed serve.

Finally, the Vietnam Women's Memorial is a symbol of healing. It is an opportunity to recognize and be proud of our contribution, acknowledge the impact of the experience on our lives and those close to us, and to move on.

There may be scars but given the proper care and attention, wounds do heal.

The Vietnam Women's Memorial is a beautiful tribute to all women who served during the Vietnam era, a vivid reminder of the lessons we learned, and I pray shall never forget, and a celebration of patriotism, courage, caring, and healing.

The Wall: Facts and Figures

Although everyone knows it as the Wall, the monument's official name is the Vietnam Veterans Memorial. Not the Vietnam Memorial or the Vietnam War Memorial—the Vietnam Veterans Memorial. As those of us who were involved in its creation insisted, it is a monument not to war but to all those who served in a war—those who made it home as well as those who did not.

The Wall is actually two walls, each stretching for 246.75 feet and joined at an angle of 125 degrees. They seem to rise up out of the ground and reach a height of 10.1 feet at the vertex.

Architect Maya Ying Lin's stunning design was chosen from a competition of 1,421 entries. Initially, it was surrounded by controversy, but that controversy all but disappeared as the Wall was built and opened to the public. Much of the controversy is attributed to the difficulty in capturing the true feel of the Memorial in two-dimensional print. As anyone who has ever been knows, it has to be seen in person to be experienced.

Each wall contains 70 panels of black granite that was mined in India and polished to a brightness that reflects not only the individual looking at the Wall but the sky and the ground as well.

Where the two walls come together in the middle, the first panel meets the last. The first person killed in Vietnam meets the last one to die.

On November 11, 1984, The Three Servicemen Statue was added. Commissioned by VVMF, the sculpture by Frederick Hart portrays a representative sample of Americans who served in Vietnam.

The most recent—and final—addition to the Vietnam Veterans Memorial is the Vietnam Women's Memorial, depicting the contributions made by women in Vietnam, including a nurse holding a wounded soldier in her arms.

58,191 Names

But it is the Wall that is the focal point. And the names it carries—58,191 of them. At the top of Panel 1 East, the Memorial is dedicated thusly:

> In honor of the men and women of the Armed Forces of the United States who served in the Vietnam War. The names of those who gave their lives and those who remain missing, are inscribed in the order they were taken from us.

Determining and verifying the names was a monumental undertaking in itself. At first the criteria for a name to be included were simple. Executive Orders from Presidents Johnson and Nixon had specified Vietnam, Laos, Cambodia and coastal areas as a combat zone.

This was later expanded to include those killed in air crashes enroute to or returning from combat missions.

The Department of Defense makes the determinations and many times the choice to include or not include is difficult. Many cases were heartbreaking. Some were in comas. Some had died during training or on their way to Indochina. There were still others who had committed suicide shortly after their return home from Southeast Asia.

The procedure was painstaking. Under the direction of Robert Doubek, the Vietnam Veterans Memorial Fund spent several months crosschecking casualty lists to make sure every eligible name was included.

A further two-month effort went into guaranteeing that each name was spelled correctly. The VVMF paid to have the personnel at the Military Personnel Records Center in St. Louis pull out each fatality's individual folder and double-check the spelling of his or her name on the final fatality list.

Names of casualties who have died since the war

have been added as necessary since 1983.

In Memorium

It almost seems remarkable that no one is actually buried at the Wall. A casual visitor who did not know better could certainly assume that there are veterans buried there.

One factor that helps feed that impression is the unending array of memorabilia left behind by visitors to the Wall. Since it was first dedicated, nearly 30,000 objects and artifacts, ranging from handwritten notes on popsicle sticks to oil paintings, have been left at the Wall.

There is a story that, as the foundation for the Memorial was being poured in 1982, a man came up to the workmen pouring the concrete.

He said he and his brother were aircraft pilots in Vietnam and he carried a Purple Heart that had been awarded to his brother who had died in Vietnam. He asked the workers if they would mind if he threw it into the foundation.

No one minded, so he did. Then he stepped back, saluted his dead brother and said, "Now the Memorial has a heart."

Since then, medals galore have been left at the Wall, purple hearts, bronze stars, almost any award imaginable. On the morning of the 10th Anniversary of the Vietnam Veterans Memorial, someone left a Congressional Medal of Honor at the Wall.

Everything is kept. The National Park Service wherever possible tries to track down the story behind some of the more unusual offerings.

Some are obviously debts repaid, a can of beer ("here's the drink I owe you. 24 years late."), a pack of cigarettes.

Someone in fact once left 12 beers and two packs of Kool-Aid. Park officials later determined that a vet left it for the 14 buddies he lost in Vietnam—12 beers for the guys who drank and Kool-Aid for the two who did not.

There's a teddy bear with the name tags of buddies sewn on it. Champagne glasses, baby booties, flowers, flags, pacifiers, dog tags, poetry, personal letters, model ships, planes and cars, toy soldiers, key chains, t-shirts, travel kits, flight jackets, other articles of military clothing.

Many times a visitor will encounter what amounts to a shrine, where a friend or loved one has placed a photograph of the deceased servicemember in a frame with flowers around it and a candle burning.

Each item is obviously intensely personal and this memorabilia is an integral part of the Vietnam Veterans Memorial experience.

Random Observations and Comments IV

Henry A. Kissinger, former U.S. Secretary of State

The Wall is a fitting memorial to the more than three million Americans who served in the Vietnam War. The millions of people, young and old, who visit the Wall each year cannot help but be moved by the eloquence of its silence and the sad beauty of its message. The Wall has become a place of compassion and a monument to healing.

It is to the healing that all Americans must now turn their attention. No struggle since the Civil War has so riven our people. No issue has raised such passions.

As a nation we must put those divisions behind us, recognizing that honorable men and women honestly disagreed over our nation's course. In its stark and somber beauty, the Vietnam Veterans Memorial can help bring about a reconciliation of which all Americans can be proud.

Diane Carlson Evans, Chair and Founder of the Vietnam Women's Project

" . . . as clerks stood in the doorway of the X-ray room betting on how long I would live; my most vivid and fondest memory is of her . . . in a soft and caring voice, she took and cradled my left hand in hers and all she said was, you're all right . . . that single act of her unselfish concern generated within me the greatest will to live; that is what I remember most about that day, July 22, 1969, Vietnam."

The story of the Vietnam War is one of courage and sacrifice of American men and women. But how many people realized that during the tumultuous period of Vietnam women volunteered to serve?

For years, these invisible women veterans were silent. But their silence did not quiet the hearts of tens of thousands of American soldiers and their families who understood the value of women's important and dedicated service.

During the Vietnam War, women who joined the military effort—more than 265,000—were invaluable to their brother and sister soldiers, yet unknown to their nation.

Women worked with skill and courage behind the scenes, off camera and off the record. Eight of them have their names etched on the "Wall."

Throughout history the media, art and memorials have focused on the men who fight wars. But now for the first time in our nation a memorial honoring American military women has been placed in Washington, D.C.—on the site of the Vietnam Veterans Memorial.

The bronze multifigure sculpture portrays women as they looked in Vietnam—and reflects their service with bravery, compassion and strength.

Silent no more, veterans and thousands of Americans came to Washington, D.C. on Veterans Day 1993 to the dedication of the Vietnam Women's Memorial to say "thank you" to all those who gave so much.

Fr. Theodore M. Hesburgh

As a member of the selection committee for those proposing models for the Vietnam Veterans Memorial in Washington, I was struck by the simplicity of the design chosen. I wished that the ultimate solution to the problems of Vietnam Veterans could be so simple.

The monument, with all its stark simplicity, did help. It was there. The thousands of names of the fallen warriors were there.

People came in large numbers to stand and contemplate, to find the name of a comrade or friend, to pray for the repose of their souls, in a way, to welcome them home.

That was a good beginning. But, as Lincoln said in his Gettysburg address, the real problem is with the living — the still suffering survivors of Vietnam. They too, must, at long last, be welcomed home. That is beginning to happen, thank God.

As long as the memorial stands there, we are reminded of our unfinished business. The war will be forgotten but those who suffered and died there, in America's most unpopular war, deserve our respect, our help, and all the measure of honor we can pay them.

As the up-until-now unsung heroes who carried the national burden, and carried it mostly alone, and often still do, we owe our abiding respect and thanks.

Michael Shannon Davison, General U.S. Army (Ret.)

The creation of this memorial was not easy. Even amongst those of us who had served in Vietnam, there was division. The Wall, in spite of its eloquent simplicity of design, stirred immediate discussion, debate and demand.

Yet, there proved to be a common thread that ran through the rancorous rhetoric — the Memorial should honor not just those who lost their lives, but all who answered the call of their country, put on the uniform and went to Vietnam. Thus, the

Statue was born.

The Statue speaks as eloquently as does the Wall. For those who have been in combat, the three figures by their posture and expressions reflect that mystic bond of love that surrounds those in battle who are at constant grave risk and who depend upon each other for their very lives. So, I find the Statue to be deeply moving.

No less so is the Wall. It too speaks. The polished black stone not only reflects the respectful visitors who pass in front of it but also reaches out to bring into its reflection the trees and the clouds and the sky.

Thus, it surrounds the names of those who gave their lives with nature's tribute as well as the tribute of those who come to honor the departed heroes.

Robert M. Kimmitt, former U.S. Ambassador to the Federal Republic of Germany

The dedication of the Vietnam Veterans Memorial represented a significant milestone in the very important process of healing that our nation has undergone since the end of the conflict in Southeast Asia.

As a veteran of this conflict who served an extended combat tour with the 173rd Airborne Brigade, I feel a personal bond with the many

Americans who died, or who lost friends or family members, during this very difficult period.

Indeed, the Memorial contains the names of many soldiers who died at my side, as well as the names of seventeen of my West Point classmates who made the ultimate sacrifice for freedom.

Those who worked hard to see such a memorial built and those who continue their support have made the Vietnam Veterans Memorial a living monument to the memories of the many men and women who fell in this conflict.

They have provided an invaluable service to their nation by assuring that all Americans— regardless of their political views—have a place to come together in reconciliation.

Americans are deeply indebted to those who served so bravely and selflessly in Southeast Asia.

I urge you all to continue the process of healing.

Jimmy Carter, 39th President of the United States

Certainly the recovery process is not over; there will always be scars for anyone affected—directly or indirectly—by the Vietnam War. The Wall reminds us of those who served, and of our commitment to the pursuit of lasting world peace.

Charles Mathias, former U.S. Senator from Maryland

The concept of a memorial to honor veterans of the war in Vietnam unified the United States Senate! Very rarely do all of the one hundred Senators join together in introducing a legislative proposal, but they did so for Vietnam veterans.

They were prescient in recognizing and representing the sentiment of the overwhelming majority of Americans who wanted to extend heart and hand to the men and women who had fought in the jungles of southeast Asia.

This message is embodied in the stone of the Wall and has been felt by every visitor who stood before it in the years it has enhanced the Mall in Washington.

Charles T. Hagel, Vietnam Veteran

Vietnam crippled some of America's self confidence and clouded its manifest destiny. The long years of confusing struggle ripped the fabric of a society born of a generous nation and magnanimous people.

The arrival of the abstract and poignantly different memorial dedicated to the memory of those who fought and died in an abstract and poignantly different war, brought an openness of expression and reflection that allowed a national and personal healing to begin.

It came to be called the Wall. Simple, elegant, provocative and to-the-point, this manifestation of remembrance reached out to the soul of who we are as Americans; our beliefs, our differences and our love of country.

Few times in our brief national history has there been a "thing" that so moved a nation. The Wall is many statements . . . it represents many perspectives, many ideas, and many emotions. There is no glory in war—only sorrow.

The Wall represents sorrow—but it also represents inspiration, faith, sacrifice, love and the fragility of life.

The Wall is what none of us can adequately express in words. The Wall is what each of us wants it to be, and feels in our heart it is.

A Personal Journey of Healing

Rev. Philip G. Salois, M.S.
President, National Conference of Vietnam
Veteran Ministers

My first visit to the Wall was the result of a therapeutic homework assignment culminating a six-month intense outpatient treatment program for Post Traumatic Stress Disorder.

I was in my final year of preparation for ordination to the Priesthood when 13 years of pent-up war-time memories burst through the door of my Vietnam "closet."

The date of March 1, 1970, was the focal point not only of my trauma but also the genesis of my vocational call. March 1st—I, a rifleman in the 2nd Platoon of the 3rd Battalion, 7th Infantry of the 199th Light Infantry Brigade, marched right into a numerically superior force of NVA entrenched in an elaborate bunker complex.

A U-shaped ambush awaited us. A major firefight broke out. Six men leading out the platoon were immediately separated from the rest of our element. Fear and rage overtook me in the long wait for rescue attempts to the separated element.

In desperation, I made a hasty battlefield promise to God for my safety and protection. I initiated a rescue mission to help the six men. The mission was completed and successful but in the process a round which had no one's name on it struck my buddy, Herb Klug, in the head—a round which could just as easily have been meant for me.

July 4, 1984—First Visit to the Wall

One month after my priestly ordination, I made my first pilgrimage to Washington. Panel 13-West, Line 70 and 71—the names of Herb Klug from Dayton, Ohio, and on the line above, Terrence Bowell, our platoon leader, one of the six whose lives ended that day, glared at me at eye level.

In a quiet stupor, I gazed at those names amidst hundreds of people likewise paying their respects. I wanted to cry—felt it was the appropriate thing to do—yet could not bring myself to tears; they came much later in the year following and in private.

I was forever changed by that visit. No longer could I conceal in a "closet" what the Vietnam War had done to me.

The repressed feelings of anger, rage, sadness, grief, guilt and shame were like a gaping open wound making me vulnerable to the emotional roller coaster I would be riding in subsequent years.

To quote liberally from the words of Maya Lin, that day at the Wall began for me, " . . . a journey, a journey that would experience death" (from <u>To Heal A Nation</u>), and " . . . bring (me) to a point . . . to an awareness . . . that (I, as an individual have) to turn around and walk back up into the light and that's where the hope and the healing comes from." (passim from the videotape <u>All the Unsung Heroes</u>).

In retrospect and reflection, I realize today the impact the Wall has had on my life. It brings to life the passage from the Gospel of St. John (12:24) when Jesus says, " . . . unless the grain of wheat fall to the earth and dies, it remains just a grain of wheat. But if it dies, it produces much fruit."

It took the Wall to make me realize that was the gift of life Herb gave to me that day—to wash away my guilt for his dying that I might live and keep his memory alive in the work that I have been entrusted—the ministry of healing and reconciliation to Vietnam Veterans and their families.

The Journey of Healing—Personal Process

This journey of healing begun at the Wall has led me:

- May 1989, to establish a personal ministry to Vietnam Veterans and their families.
- November 1989, to found a national organization of Vietnam Clergy, the

National Conference of Vietnam Veteran
Ministers.

— June 1990, to make a return trip to Vietnam
   with other veterans for the purpose of personal healing and reconciliation.

— November 1990, to the first gathering of
   Vietnam Clergy with a candlelight service
   at the Wall.

— July 1991, to visit for the first time Herb's
   parents and his gravesite in Dayton, Ohio.

— September 1991, to sponsor and receive a
   Vietnamese refugee family with two Amera-
   sian children to the U.S. I had met this family while on my return trip to Vietnam the
   previous year.

In brief, all these things I attribute to the spiritual
energy which emanated from the Wall which was
infused in me on that Fourth of July, 1984.

A celebration of true freedom and liberation.

Random Observations and Comments V

Anonymous, Houston, Texas

I was born in 1967 and have only dim memories of news reports about the war. I didn't know anybody who fought in the war—my dad did his military service in the '50s and my uncles were too young. I never thought much about it except when I got older and learned about some of the reasons why the U.S. got involved; about things like the bombing of Laos and Cambodia, etc. I thought (and still do) that it was a mistake. But I never thought about the people who went there. On a school trip in 1984, I went to Washington and saw the Memorial. Its stark form, all the names, the flowers and mementos people left there—it had a deep effect on me. I found out about the POW/MIAs who might still be there, about how poorly the returning veterans were treated both by the U.S. public and by the government, about the problems of depression, homelessness, suicide. Well, the point of all of this is that I would like to thank you. For going, for coming back, and for the work you have done to bring these issues to the attention of the public. I just saw you speaking on Nightline about Lew Puller, Jr. and you mentioned something he had said to President Bush, ''I am healed, but there are a lot of guys out there who aren't.'' I hope that these men and women get the recognition, help and the thanks they deserve. They have my respect and my thanks.

Alan L. Gropman, Colonel USAF (Retired)

The genius of the Vietnam Veterans Memorial—the Wall—is the names. To those of us who served and lost comrades, the display of the names makes the memorial intensely meaningful, genuine and tangible.

I know it is the same for those who did not serve, but lost someone they remember. And I also know the display of the names makes the Memorial significant even for those who knew not one of the more than 58,000 names carved on the black marble [granite].

The names make the Wall explicit in human terms.

When I stand at the junction of the two wings in the center of the memorial, I sense that I am with companions.

I am not melancholy, and my bearing is not

funereal. How can it be, I am among comrades.
I forget entirely—if only momentarily—the bit-
terness and political turmoil over the Vietnam War
and focus entirely on those with whom I served—
my friends.

When I visit the Wall I always touch the name
of a lost comrade and that touching creates an
intense memory in my mind of that person who
died twenty or more years ago.

I remember the camaraderie, the esprit d' corps,
the sense of belonging to something important
where self sacrifice was what was expected. The
Vietnam Veterans Memorial is an emotional balm
and a superbly fitting monument to those who
served.

Gerald R. Ford, 38th President of the United States

The Wall has tremendously affected our people
and our nation in a number of different ways. It
has given to those who lost in Vietnam a beloved
son, daughter, or intimate friend, a holy place to
pay solemn tribute or to express heartfelt, tearful
sorrow.

To those who comprehensively honor all who
served our nation in Vietnam, the Wall is where
the ultimate sacrifice in patriotism can be appro-
priately recognized.

The Wall has also been a memorial where those

who opposed the war can offer their highest
respect for those who died serving their nation.

There is something very special about the Wall.
The long, tragic conflict in Vietnam was different
from any military conflict in the history of
America. Vast public differences on U.S. government policy dominated the news media.

It was not a typical period in America's history.
The Wall, during its ten years, has created a con-
structive sentiment of reconciliation among those
with diverse views.

Obviously, the Wall has earned a most unique
recognition—a decade of healing. We should be
proud of its achievements for a better understanding among all Americans.

Admiral E. R. Zumwalt, Jr. (Ret.)

On the occasion of the 10th Anniversary of the
Vietnam Veterans Memorial, I join with many
others in sending greetings and heart-felt appreciation for the past and continuing sacrifices made
on behalf of our country.

I have recently had the thrill of greeting here
in Washington my war-time comrade and opposite
number, Rear Admiral Tran Van Chon, leader of
the dramatic expansion of the Vietnamese Navy,
who paid for his patriotism with twelve years in
prison in Hanoi.

This experience has driven home to me the fact

that millions of our Vietnamese compatriots have paid prices similar to or worse than our own.

I promise to dedicate myself to continuing efforts to obtain recognition by our government of its responsibility to American veterans of Vietnam.

I ask that you join me in showing that our government does not forget our Vietnamese counterparts whose suffering also continues.

Reflections of a Gold Star Mother

Violet C. Long, former National President
American Gold Star Mothers, Inc.

When I said goodbye to our son Charles that cold morning in January, 1969, little did I realize it would be the last time I would see him again and in nine months I would be a Gold Star Mother.

His death was difficult for me to accept. I never lost hope that perhaps it wasn't true until all the troops were home, and then I knew I had to face reality.

In 1971, I was invited to join the American Gold Star Mothers organization. As each year passed, I became more involved in the activities, and felt at ease with the other mothers in the chapter.

It was not until Gold Star Mothers Day in 1986 that I first visited the Memorial. As I walked slowly along the Wall, I suddenly realized I was not—and never was—alone in my grief.

More than 50,000 parents had experienced the same tragedy of the loss of a precious young son or daughter.

At that moment, the healing began. Now when

I visit the Memorial, I still feel sadness for the loss of the many young lives, but I can also reflect, not on what could have been for that is painful, but I remember vividly my first look at Charles when he was born (he could have been a football player); his love of food equalled that of his father's; honesty was one of his finest qualities (he would call me at the office to tell me he didn't make it to school that day because he overslept); his desire for a 1957 Chevy was number one on his "wish" list, and I will never forget Debby, his first love.

Today, I find there is comfort in Remembrance; healing in Reflection. I found it at the Wall.

"I Tell Them I'm Sorry"

Travis Ryan, former U.S. Army Reservist

I remember vividly my first visit to the Wall. It was not planned. I was in Washington on a business trip and one of the people I was working with, a friend, talked me into going.

I'll be honest. I was uneasy. Uncertain. After all, I had my own memories of Vietnam and those who went there and I wasn't sure how those memories and I would "fit in" with others who would be at the Wall.

In truth (although maybe it's just because I hope there's safety in numbers), I think a great many Americans have somewhat the same experience, the same troubled, confused, memories about that war that divided our nation for what seemed like forever.

At the beginning, our involvement seemed right. Of course, I was a young Irish Catholic who believed President Kennedy could do no wrong. I bought the "domino theory" and believed America needed to help South Vietnam defend itself against the communist onslaught from the North.

When did those feelings, those beliefs, change? What caused the change? I can't point to any one thing. There were several.

One was my aunt, a favorite relative of mine. She worked for the Selective Service and had done so for most of her working career.

The agony of calling young men into the Army and sending them over to Vietnam where so many died so quickly, became too much for her to bear. She took early retirement, rather than continue to live with the terrible feelings her job placed upon her.

She confided her anguish to me. She also confided that she was concerned about me. That made two of us.

At that time, like every other male my age, I grew up knowing that I owed my country a time in the service. There was no lottery yet, no "lucky number" drawing. That would come later.

I did have a college deferment that would carry me through June of 1966. I planned to get married right after that, and I kept hearing rumors about married men being dropped lower in draft sequences. But I wasn't about to count on that possibility to keep me from being drafted. Nor could I look to my aunt for help. As I said, military service was a part of life, something we had to accept.

But I was lucky. I placed my name on the waiting list for the U.S. Army Reserve. The list

cleared and I was enlisted as a "weekend warrior."

The training schedule was such that it was
almost a year later, in the summer of 1967, before
I was called up for my Active Duty training. I was
sent to Fort Polk, Louisiana.

Fort Polk when I was there was basically divided
in half. South Fort housed most of the troops in
basic training and for advanced training in other
than combat infantry roles. North Fort was one
of the Army's primary training grounds for
Vietnam-bound troops.

An Advanced Infantry Training assignment to
North Fort was almost a lock-tight guarantee that
you'd be going to Vietnam.

I knew where I'd be going when my Advanced
Training was over. Home. Throughout that hot,
blistering summer, that was an extremely comforting thought. Yet I couldn't help but feel guilty as
well.

As basic training concluded, I watched one after
another of my fellow platoon members open their
orders and see their assignment to North Fort.
Many broke down and cried. So many of them
were so young, it was very difficult. They were
scared, truly scared. And I was scared for them.

After I returned home and resumed my "weekend warrior" role, the anti-war protests began to
mount. Ironically, our Reserve unit was designated
for riot control training, and we spent many of our

weekends drilling and preparing in case we were needed.

Remembering the faces of my fellow basic trainees wondering how many of them might have already been killed, I went through riot control training, moving in tight formation, with bayonet fixed—and with part of me always feeling like I was just as likely to be on the other side of that bayonet as I was on this side.

Yet I enjoyed my years in the Reserve. Even thought seriously about re-enlisting when my six years were up. But I didn't.

As I approached the Wall that day, however, it wasn't my "illustrious" six years in the Reserves that was on my mind. It was more like "what right do I have to be here? Change any of a number of things and my name could be on that Wall with someone standing here looking for it."

I felt guilty. Not necessarily ashamed, but guilty. I had done nothing illegal. I didn't even have family influence or money to use. I just was lucky. And it was that luck that made me feel guilty as I approached the Wall.

The Wall and the people there.

I stared, and I saw plenty. I listened, and I heard nothing. Silence. Reverence. Respect. It was all around me.

Where my friend was who brought me there, I had no idea. He was gone, at least as far as I was concerned. I was in another world, a new world.

I went looking for no names in particular. Then I did. A schoolmate from my high school days, one of the first from my home town to die in that war. We weren't what anyone would call good friends, but we knew each other and would talk to each other.

I found his name. And we talked once again.

Then I began looking for some of those kids from Fort Polk. Trying to remember roll calls, name after name that came into mind, I tracked down and couldn't find. Then I'd find one. And another. Four in all. I was embarrassed that sometimes it was so hard to put a face with a name. I traced the corners of my mind for memories, barracks, formations, PE runs—then I'd remember.

As I did, I thought about how badly I felt for this person I had known for all of six weeks. And I thought about his family, his friends, and how terribly they must have felt when they received the news that had he died.

And I once again thought about and felt guilty about the luck of the draw that had left me here looking at his name instead of the other way around.

With that "baptism," I felt no longer an outsider, no longer unwelcome. I even dared to begin speaking to others there.

I was especially moved by one man, a vet, in his fatigue uniform. He told me that when he came home after the war, he felt so despised, so dirty, he moved into the mountainous woods near his home and swore never to return to "civilization."

The Wall changed his mind. When it was first dedicated, he felt he had to come, look up his buddies who had been killed, and come to peace with himself—no matter what his fellow Americans might think.

When he did, he found something totally unexpected. He found acceptance. He found peace. But he also found a cause. He told me he would stay there at the Wall until every American still "missing" in Southeast Asia was brought home.

I've made many trips to the Wall since then. Never for any specific reason, except maybe to come to an even greater peace with myself.

And when I go back, I talk. I talk to the people around me— those who indicate a willingness— and I talk to the names on the Wall.

I tell them I'm sorry. I'm sorry I ever questioned their patriotism, their manhood, their willingness to follow their country's orders.

And I walk away always with the same feeling—that if those 58,000 young Americans had lived, had been able to share with us all their knowledge, their patriotism, their indomitable spirit, what a better world this would be.

I look back toward the Wall one last time and am thankful for what it has done—for each of those names, for millions of others who served and who still don't receive the respect they deserve, for a nation in turmoil, and yes, for me.

Random Observations and Comments VI

Harry G. Robinson, III, Dean of Architecture at Howard University

War either unites or tears asunder a country and her people. When the latter occurs, the healing process requires a powerful spiritual, almost mystical centrifugal force to close the wounds of armed conflict abroad and public strife on our native shores.

History has recorded this force as a seminal speech, " . . . testing whether that Nation or any Nation so dedicated and conceived can long endure . . . ;" the legendary heroic stands of our young warriors; the charismatic one time proclamations of military leaders; and endings laced with national rituals embodying victory and its rites.

The war in Vietnam had few of these and none that endeared it or us to our country. Instead, our war eroded the moral authority and spiritual center of this great land. Our collective conscience carried the pain of that erosion no matter how pure and valiant our individual intentions and merits.

Ten years after its dedication, the Vietnam Veterans Memorial, our memorial, "The Wall," stands for and has absorbed the pain and grieving of our generation's comrades-in-arms, that of their families, and that of a Nation shaken at its foundations by the loss of its sense of self and some of its pilgrimage to pay homage to our generation, its living and its dead, to those who returned to our soil and to those left behind.

The Wall is our victory, the Nation's victory, our closure. It has achieved what we couldn't. It has won the "hearts and minds" of Americans.

It's over.

Country Joe McDonald, Musician

The Vietnam Veterans Memorial in Washington, DC, is the only touchstone the Vietnam War generation has to let us know that it was not a nightmare but was real.

As the majority of the generation and the rest of "the world" go about their business as if nothing happened. As if there is no need to rethink our values and goals. As if there is no need to grieve.

We, the weak and the verbal come to the Wall to find ourselves by paying respect to a small portion of those who paid the ultimate price for a foreign policy run amok.

There are those who rail against the Wall and the generation, but we did not effect government policy then . . . we were just children and young adults who did the best we could in a terrible situation that seemed as if it would never end.

There will be no "coming home" until home is safe to come to. Almost all Americans are "homeless" today. Some physically, some mentally and some spiritually . . . but "homeless" just the same. We went off to war and did not really come back home because home had changed and we had changed.

Until the day we "find ourselves" again as a country, we, the Vietnam War generation have the Vietnam Veterans Memorial as a place to go to remember and reflect upon our own lives, our family, our friends and our country.

And to grieve.

Liz Trotta, TV War Correspondent

This Wall rose not in the flush of victory, or in the fullness of a nation's ready gratitude. It staggered into majesty by the power of its remembrance, long after the dead had earned their place on its mirrored face, long after America had buried them in its shuddering soul.

What a miracle that it stands at all. Those who know the names come to find and honor them, weeping before the silence of the brave.

But where are those who in that dark age heard the call to arms and turned away? To protest, to flee, to erase the memory. And if one day they stand to face its marble [granite] truth, what will they say?

George McGovern, former U.S. Senator

What a marvelous role the Vietnam Veterans Memorial has played. How could we have better captured the tragedy and the glory of a conflict that so gripped the nation for so many years.

As early as 1963, when I was a freshman member of the U.S. Senate, I came to the conclusion that our military involvement in the Vietnamese civil war was a mistake. I am all the more certain of that judgment now.

But always I have honored the sacrifice and the suffering of the brave Americans who fought in Vietnam. The conflict in Vietnam was chartered by America's political leadership—not by the men who fought there.

I salute those men, and the women who were there, for their courage, their patriotism and their sacrifice.

The Vietnam Veterans Memorial, with its permanently inscribed listing of the names of our soldiers, will forever remind us that we have an obligation of immense importance to assist and appreciate and understand our Vietnam veterans.

I have always believed that those of us who opposed American policy in Vietnam have a special
obligation to embrace the Americans who fought
in that conflict as well as those who, in good conscience, could not support the war.

It is also past time for America to stretch out
a healing hand to the long suffering people of
Vietnam.

Robert G. Stanton, Director, National Capital Region, National Park Service

No memorial in recent history has become so
popular so quickly or become the destination for
so many visitors to the Nation's Capital.

No memorial in the last 50 years since the
Thomas Jefferson Memorial was dedicated by
President Franklin Roosevelt has so altered our
concept of what a memorial should be and how
powerfully it can move the heart and grace the
landscape.

The story of the Vietnam Veterans Memorial
is told every day on the faces of thousands of
visitors who file past its black granite walls.

The memorial raises a flood of memories.
Thousands of letters, photos and objects have been
left at the Wall and collected by the National Park
Service since the memorial was dedicated in 1982.

More than a memorial, what was created here

has become a special place of pilgrimage. It stands as a symbol of America's long-awaited welcome home to those who served in Vietnam.

Once that welcome was heard and understood, we could begin to heal the wounds and close this anguished chapter in our history.

The National Park Service reconfirms its support of the founding organization, the Vietnam Veterans Memorial Fund, and its worthy efforts.

As administrators of the memorial, the National Park Service is dedicated to honor the memory of those who served and died in Vietnam.

We pledge to keep faith with their families and friends who visit here. And we applaud the efforts of Vietnam veterans who continue to give their best to America.

Veterans Organizations Reflect on the Wall

**Robert W. Spanogle, National Adjutant
The American Legion**

My personal memories of the Vietnam Veterans Memorial date from the late 1970s, when Jan Scruggs wrote the National Commander of The American Legion for support of the Memorial.

I was given the assignment as The American Legion's liaison to the Vietnam Veterans Memorial Fund.

As a Vietnam-era veteran, my memories surrounding the Memorial are as follows: Courage, persistence and healing.

Courage that the Vietnam Veterans Memorial was built against formidable odds; the persistence of Jan Scruggs, the Vietnam Veterans Memorial Fund and the veterans community that its building was a just cause; but above all, the healing effect of the Memorial and the message it gives to Vietnam veterans and the nation.

In my view, the Memorial commemorates the sacrifice of those of our generation who gave their lives, but it also remembers those yet to return and recognizes those still suffering.

The Wall is a constant reminder of the young men and women who served their country in America's most divisive war.

The Vietnam Veterans Memorial Fund and those of us who stood with it overcame a mean-spirited opposition—some motivated by ego and others who bowed to petty politics.

Bringing the Vietnam Veterans Memorial into reality was not easy, nor was it pleasant, much like the Vietnam War itself.

In the end, however, the Memorial is a reflection of a generation of Americans who served honorably and with courage. Perhaps my life's greatest honor was being a part of the building of the Memorial.

My thanks go out to the 3.1 million members of The American Legion who, through their average donation of $8, raised $1.3 million for the construction of the Memorial.

The dedication of the Wall began the reconciliation and understanding of the Vietnam Veteran community with the nation.

Joseph C. Zengerle, National Commander, Disabled American Veterans

I am grateful for this opportunity to honor the Vietnam Veterans Memorial.

As National Commander of the Disabled American Veterans, I can express the shared commitment of over 1.2 million members, disabled in wartime military service since World War I.

As a Vietnam veteran, I recall with pride when, as assistant secretary of the Air Force in 1980, I set aside a hangar at Andrews Air Force Base for the conduct of the Memorial's design competition.

In 1982 — on the eve of the dedication of the Memorial — America was a land not yet ready to confront the pain generated by the Vietnam War.

Vietnam veterans were anonymous in our society, and without an apparent voice in the nation. "Let's forget that divisive war," America needed to say. But to forget the war, America would have to forget the people who fought in it — its own sons and daughters.

When it was dedicated, the Vietnam Veterans Memorial immediately declared it was a place that would not let America forget. The names of those in Southeast Asia, etched in black granite, became a focal point for introspection, for dialogue, and — ultimately — for healing.

Americans know this, and have flocked to the Memorial in record numbers ever since. They have joined together here to honor the memory of those who fell in combat, and to celebrate the lives of those who came home.

The Vietnam Veterans Memorial — a place for

all of us to remember how dear our freedoms are, and how fearful a price their preservation exacts.

Larry W. Rivers, Executive Director, Veterans of Foreign Wars of the United States

No monument, no memorial has had more of a profound impact on a nation and its people as this reflective black marble [granite] slab with the names of friends, comrades and loved ones.

The names etched in this black stone represent the finest of my generation.

They answered the call—as did countless Americans of generations past—believing that certain truths and certain bedrock American principles were worth fighting and bleeding and even dying for.

Since the Vietnam War, we have, as a nation, learned a great deal about our strengths and fallibilities. Let us be judicious in using our strength and equally mindful of our fallibilities.

It is my hope that my fellow Vietnam veterans and I will be remembered not as veterans who fought a losing war but rather as American patriots who were willing to put our very lives on the line despite the timidity and loss of will of political leaders entrusted with providing a just and moral basis for our sacrifice.

Today, let this peaceful place remind us that war and the terrible price it extracts can no longer be an acceptable way to settle disputes among men of good will.

Shad Meshad, President of the National Veterans Foundation

1992 is the 10th Anniversary of the Vietnam Veterans Memorial. As I reflect back over this historic occasion, memories of healing and coming together bring back the most powerful, immediate emotions.

The Wall and the VA Outreach Program started about the same time as far as concept and development—the late 70s and early 80s. Both emerged from a critical need to work through and heal from the Vietnam War. Both worked in collaboration to achieve this task: many Vet Center clients, both alone and in groups, visited the Wall as a means of healing.

This has continued since for the past 10 years. Just as the Vet Centers provided free readjustment to all Vietnam Veterans as a way of getting on with their lives and approaching the highest potential, so too does the Wall.

It is no exaggeration to say that there can be no effective healing of Post Traumatic Stress Disorder for great numbers of Vietnam Vets without considerable attention given to the spiritual, moral and religious dimension of combat related stress.

The Wall has certainly provided healing for

veterans and for the larger society. It is almost a
religious symbol.

The Wall embodies the rediscovery and meaning through a physical symbol of a tragic event.
Farewells uttered to loved ones and friends, healing of spiritual hurts, and reconnection with society
can all take place at the Wall because it is a
material, tangible reality that symbolizes a much
larger dimension of being.

" . . . like visiting the great cathedrals of Europe."

Sean Thomas, Richmond, Virginia

There's a very special feeling you get when you visit the Wall. It took a long time for me to come up with words to describe it. Finally it hit me.

It's like visiting the great cathedrals of Europe. You enter the Memorial area and immediately you're struck by a feeling of majesty, a sense of being overwhelmed by your surroundings, much the same way you are when you enter a great church.

As you tear your eyes away from the Wall itself, you look at the people around you. And you begin to worry that you're disturbing their worship. You're there as a tourist, a curious individual, not drawn for any specific mission or purpose.

But those other people are not. They're here to pay respects to, to communicate with, a loved one, a relative or a buddy. Their focus is intense, strong, and you feel uneasy, begin shifting your feet as well as your eyes, to make sure you don't block someone's view, interrupt their meditation.

You glance around you at the offerings people have left, personal possessions, flowers, notes, almost anything and everything you can imagine—and the feeling is much like the votive candles people light in those cathedrals, as they pray in memory of a loved one, a relative, a buddy.

While you know there is real grief around you, you don't feel it, don't sense its presence. Instead, it's as if you've walked into an atmosphere of peace and comfort and tranquility.

People are talking, you can see them. But somehow you don't hear them. The silence too, is comforting, not smothering or disturbing. And it all seems almost strange until you finally realize what has happened.

You're no longer just a tourist, a curiosity seeker. You're a participant in this service that is going on all around you.

Your eyes return again and again to the Wall. What just a few minutes ago (or was it hours? Time does strange things here.) was an overwhelming edifice of polished black granite that seemed to stretch forever has become an intensely personal experience instead.

You no longer see thousands of names. Instead you see one name, then another, then another. You find yourself envisioning the person represented by that name. How old was he? How did it happen? What must the agony have been like for his parents, his wife, or his children when they learned the terrible news?

Is one of these people nearby a relative? Do they know him? Could you ask about him? No.

You leave them alone, move on to other names and ask yourself the same questions. They're not names anymore, they're people. Young people. Men and women. Oh, boys and girls, many of them, but the experiences they had been through before they were killed made them men and women.

It may not be prayer. It may not have anything to do with religion. It has everything to do with respect. If you came here neutral, with no feelings about the Vietnam War one way or the other. If you came here believing the war and those who fought in it were right or if you came here believing the opposite, it no longer matters.

Whatever you felt about the war no longer matters. It's that name you're staring at that counts. And the person it represents. And that person's family, loved ones and friends.

A conversion has taken place. That name you're looking at belongs to someone whose country called and who said "Yes, I'll go."

And who made the ultimate sacrifice as a result.

The change is now complete. It is like being in one of the greatest cathedrals in Europe. But you're no longer out of place, no longer an outsider. You're now one of those whom other people are reluctant to interrupt.

And you find yourself looking for newcomers, so you can make them feel as welcome, as part of all this, as you do.

Yes, there's a very special feeling you get when you visit the Wall.

Reflections in Verse

The Wall
Alneta Knowles, Poplar Bluff, Missouri

Oh Mother Earth your battlefields
Overflowed with red
The scars of memory still remain
Where your native sons have bled.
Grieving wives and mothers
Drop tears upon your crust
I see your gallant soldiers
Lying silent in the dust.

There's a Monument in Washington
Erected as a shrine
To honor all those many men
Who died on the battleline.
And from each fallen comrade
Freedom's Road was paved
Many come to see "The Wall"
And touch the names engraved.

A father comes to pay respects
A mother kneels to pray
Friends embrace with tear-filled eyes
Someone leaves a flower spray.

A teddybear left by a child
Lies limp upon the dirt
As many wartime buddies
Pour out their pain and hurt.

There's just something about it
It affects all those that come
And draws them like a magnet
No matter where they're from.
It's a place to express feelings
A haven for us all
And those who come are not the same
Once they've seen "The Wall."

The Vietnam Veterans Memorial
Was constructed with much pride
As an everlasting symbol
Of those who fought and died.
Because those men of combat
Stepped forward to obtain
Our freedom . . . their identity
In granite shall remain.

This land we see so prosperous
Was filled with blackened char
It blossomed, but it still contains
The ugly scars of war.
They paid the cost of freedom
From the sufferings withstood

And echoes from their battlecrys
Say, "Peace To Brotherhood."

The Vietnam Tragedy
James Milton Lea, USAF 1951–1954

The night was hot and sticky, the air hung heavy
    and still.
We mustered our courage with a determined will.
We cocked our guns and cleaned our sights,
Slinging them over our shoulders, we went out to
    fight.
The distant rumble of guns in the night,
Sent shivers of fear and uneasy fright.
Fifteen Marines stood armed and ready to move
    out,
The Lieutenant, young and hardened, gave the
    orders with a shout.
"Move it men!", you all know what this is about.
Our destination was somewhere over a hill,
The AK's were humming that screeching death
    shrill.
Some men were falling like flies at our feet;
God, where is the enemy we've come out here to
    meet?
Give us our night in the jungle we pray—
Get us back to camp safely we say;
Hoping for tomorrow, and that we'll see another
    day.

As we walked the edge of the forest, that had
    suddenly come alive as before,
Screeching and hollering, birds galore—
All had their sleep disturbed once more.
But, we're the ones who haven't slept in weeks,
This haunting and daunting tragedy slowly over
    me creeps.
My teeth chatter an uncontrollable dance;
My tongue is thick and dry, God, just give me one
    more chance.
Suddenly two eyes I see, staring at me in the dark;
Barking death from the muzzle and spitting fire
    with each spark.
They all seem to miss me—I'm on my face in the
    mud;
Thank God I've never experienced that white-hot
    sickening thud.
I'm saved yet again for still another night;
When all dies down, and the jungle becomes quiet.
We evacuate our buddies by the quick chopper
    flight.
They are out and gone, a quick medical ticket to
    a far away home;
We back out and start with a groan,
The same routine we've always known.
GOD, when will this 10,000 day war end?
I don't think one more day I can stand;
And still be a Marine and still be a Man.

Reflections on The Wall

They walk along The Wall,
Silent and searching,
Faces reflected in black surface,
Tears forming in eyes.

They walk along The Wall,
Silent and searching,
Intervening years
Have not quieted the pain.

They walk along The Wall,
Silent and searching,
Images of comrades
Invade the mind.

They walk along The Wall,
Silent and searching,
Seeking respite
From memories of anguish.

They walk along The Wall,
Silent and searching,
Seeking release from
Years of repudiation.

They walk along The Wall,
Silent and searching,
Outcasts of yore
In their time of need.

They walk along The Wall,
Silent and searching,
Spirits of heroes
Home, at last.

The Wall
Keith Jackson, USMC 1966–1969

From the abyss . . . came a moment in time.
From out of the past, came memories of mine.
First came your face and a name that I knew.
I had to find out what had happened to you.

Then came the day when I would find out.
Hoping to find . . . relief from my doubts.
I was given a book where answers are found.
As I stared at the book, my heart started to
    pound.

I reverently turned each page in the book.
The closer I came . . . I hesitated to look . . .
There was the TRUTH. It was open to all.
I found your name and your place on THE
    WALL.

From out of the lies, all the ruins, the cries,
Brave men that I knew now pass in review.
We still hear your laughs . . . the stories you'd
    tell.
Left are the memories of the day that you fell.

Gone are the dreams you once had of home.
Left are your NAMES . . . etched in BLACK
    STONE.
Mirrored reflections . . . of families and
    friends . . .
Numbed by the loss, still trying to mend.

One final touch. Then I reach for one more.
What was the reason why we went to war?
Despite the reason you answered the call.
I came to say THANKS to ALL on THE
    WALL.

Out of the ashes and all of the pain,
Now in my memories, you'll always remain.
Let it be known by one and all . . .
How much we THANK YOU who LIVE on
    THE WALL.

The Pied Piper

They brought us back on the freedom flight
Thirty hours ago—the jungle fight.
Leave, pass and pay—Now kill no more
Switch yourself off from the TV war.

Our debrief was "You'll get over this lot"
And so we stood in the old mascot
Home again—now that's a lark;
How many years you'll carry the spark.

The trouble years move swiftly by
And even though your loved ones try,
There's broken homes, suicide and booze.
There's strange dreams you cannot lose.

Home will be the peace of your heart
But until you're home there's no new start.
Now we'll all come home at a different rate,
But for myself, it's getting late.

So if by the mound you wish me best,
Maybe then you'll say, "he's home at rest."

Epilogue:
Jan Scruggs and His Memorial

By Michael J. Hickey

(Editor's note: No book about the Vietnam Veterans Memorial is complete without including the story of the remarkable individual who made it possible, Jan C. Scruggs. A wounded and decorated Vietnam combat infantryman, Jan Scruggs has been called the Father of the Vietnam Veterans Memorial. This is a look at the complex, often controversial, process that led to the dedication of the Wall on November 13, 1982.)

Like many Vietnam vets, Jan Scruggs suffered a sense of alienation from his own country upon his return home from that war.

Unlike many of those vets, however, he decided to do something to end that alienation. His dream, his concept was to build a memorial in Washington, D.C., that would carry the name of each and every one of the more than 58,000 Americans who had died in the Vietnam War.

Scruggs felt that too many Americans did not fully comprehend the magnitude of the sacrifice and loss involved in Vietnam and that there was a need to make that magnitude a part of our national conscience. He felt that creating a place of honor for those names would also help every Vietnam veteran "recover" from that war.

It was not an easy task. In his own words:

There was a great deal of difficulty in getting this project off the ground. First of all, hardly anyone believed that it was a worthy idea. After all, most Vietnam veterans were primarily concerned with jobs, Agent Orange and other issues relating to themselves.

I argued that the recognition a memorial would bring about would help the veterans on other issues. Everyone was skeptical, but I was totally obsessed with the idea of placing the names of all 58,000 Vietnam War deaths on the Memorial.

To realize his dream, Scruggs sold the only possession he had of real value, an inherited plot of land, and used the money ($2,800) to form the Vietnam Veterans Memorial Fund. He had VVMF incorporated and, on May 28, 1979, held a press conference, announcing plans to raise $1 million to build the memorial.

On July 4th, 1979, the Vietnam Veterans Memorial Fund made the CBS Evening News, with a mocking report that revealed that the fund had raised a grand total of $144.50.

Undaunted, Scruggs was joined by a group of dedicated volunteers. Robert Frank, George Mayo, Robert Doubek, John Woods, Jack

Wheeler, Ron Gibbs and others would contribute their time to the challenging project, and began to advance our cause.

A meeting was held with Maryland Senator Charles Mathias to develop legislation which would permit the Memorial. Virginia Senator John Warner helped get fund-raising efforts off to a good start.

But Congressional support for Scruggs' project was not unanimous to say the least.

Oh, Congress wasn't unsupportive *of the idea. A few in Congress did* catch on to *what we were trying to do, unfortunately. You see, we had put in the legislation that the Vietnam Veterans Memorial was to be placed on two acres of land next to the Lincoln Memorial. This was an outrageous and totally unreasonable demand which circumvented the standing procedures. Normally, the federal agencies select a site for memorials. We knew that we would get a site that wasn't very prominent if we used the normal procedures.*

But the boldness paid off and the site was given to VVMF on July 1, 1980, with the proviso that the project had to be complete within five years.

The controversy, however, was far from over. A competition was held to select a design for the Memorial, and a total of 1,421 entries were received. At one point, all the entries were displayed together in a mammoth hanger at Andrews Air Force base.

VVMF had assembled a jury of distinguished architects, sculptors and designers to make the selection, which VVMF could then accept or reject. The winning design was by a 21-year-old architecture student at Yale University, Maya Ying Lin—and when VVMF approved it, the controversy flared anew.

The VVMF expected some criticism no matter what sort of design we selected. Every major memorial in Washington, D.C., seemed to have caused some sort of fight. The Washington Monument had been called ugly and the work of an architect with nothing else to do. The Jefferson Memorial was called "academic, dreary and pompous" by the commission that selected its chief architect. The Lincoln Memorial had triggered bitter arguments between Northern and Southern congressmen. War memorials weren't exempt.

An organized group of veterans called the design "Black Gash of Shame and Sorrow," 'Hole in the Ground," "Sarcophagus," "Black, Flagless Pit," "Black Hole for the Dead," "Body Count on the Mall," "Wound in Mother Earth," "Open Book" and other creative, emotional names. The design selected became a sort of Rorschach inkblot test. People read almost anything into it. Much of the problem was that it was impossible to find any means to illustrate the brilliance of the design.

No two-dimensional drawing would do it justice. Even now that it has been built, one can see it on

*television, but you must make an actual visit in
order to understand the Vietnam Veterans Memorial. Since some people couldn't understand the
design, the campaign to halt its construction went
on at full steam.*

But despite efforts to derail the Memorial,
Scruggs moved ahead, fund-raising and planning.
As a compromise and to help calm some of the
critics, VVMF commissioned sculptor Frederick
Hart to do a representational sculpture of Three
Servicemen for the Memorial, and also added an
American flag.

Construction began in March of 1982 and the
dedication of the Wall took place on November
13, Veterans Day, 1982.

As one writer described the national ground-
swell, ''Jan Scruggs' dream slowly captured the
imagination of citizens across the country, fulfilling a need they had almost forgotten and releas-
ing emotions that crested on Veterans Day, 1982,
when over 15,000 Vietnam veterans gathered in
Washington for the homecoming parade they had
never had. Watching the march down Constitu-
tion Avenue, watching the hands reach out to the
Wall of names, Americans everywhere could feel
the healing power of memory begin its work.''

In the end, the Vietnam Veterans Memorial
Fund raised some $8 million—from corporations,
from unions, from veterans organizations, and
most of all, from the men, women and children

of the United States. More than 300,000 Americans made contributions, proving that the Vietnam Veterans Memorial is truly a memorial of the people.

And one man's vision fulfilled.

In the years since its dedication, the Vietnam Veterans Memorial Fund has continued working closely with the National Park Service to ensure proper maintenance of this unique and meaningful memorial. While the Park Service is responsible for the daily upkeep and maintenance—including groundskeeping and security—the Vietnam Veterans Memorial Fund has continued responsibility for its long-term maintenance and care. We do this by funding engineering studies which explore the best ways to ensure this Memorial will continue living for the generations to come, and providing financing for a diversity of needs: anything from the large-scale job of replacing the walkway to the smaller-scale purchase of the specially designed lights and directory holder parts. VVMF's mission also includes adding names and changing status (from MIA to KIA) on the Wall; providing support for the volunteer guides; co-sponsoring the annual Veterans Day and Memorial Day events; and continuing to educate about the sacrifices of those who served their country in the Vietnam War.

[ ]YES! To help the Vietnam Veterans Memorial Fund in its ongoing mission to help both the Vietnam veterans and the American people through its remarkable reconciliation process, I am enclosing my special gift of:

[ ]$25   [ ]$50   [ ]$15   [ ]$100   [ ]Other $_____

Please make check payable to Vietnam Veterans Memorial Fund and mail to: VVMF 1360 Beverly Road, #300, McLean, VA 22101-3685.

Name _____

Address _____

City/State/Zip _____

The Vietnam Veterans Memorial Fund, Inc., is a 501(c)(3) nonprofit organization eligible to receive tax-deductible donations.
THANK YOU!!